Creatures
of the
Deep

NIGEL SAMUEL

Editorial Board
David Booth • Joan Green • Jack Booth

HOUGHTON MIFFLIN HARCOURT

10801 N. Mopac Expressway
Building # 3
Austin, TX 78759
1.800.531.5015

Steck-Vaughn is a trademark of HMH Supplemental Publishers Inc.
registered in the United States of America and/or other jurisdictions.
All inquiries should be mailed to HMH Supplemental Publishers Inc.,
P.O. Box 27010, Austin, TX 78755.

Ru*bicon
www.rubiconpublishing.com

Associate Publisher: Miriam Bardswich
Editor: Dawna McKinnon
Creative/Art Director: Jennifer Drew
Cover image–Steven Hunt; title page image–Shutterstock.com

Printed in Singapore

ISBN: 978-1-4190-4021-4
8 9 10 11 12 13 14 15 16 17   2016   25 24 23 22 21 20 19 18 17 16
4500568928

CONTENTS

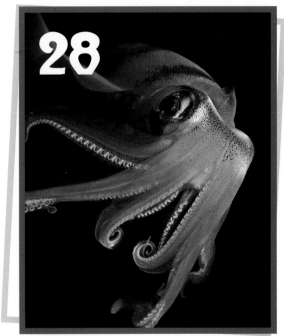

What lurks

in the depths of the great unknown —
Glowing eyes or monstrous bones?

Teeth and tentacles, scales and fins,
Mysterious creatures that
dive and swim ...

LITTLE-KNOWN

warm up

With a partner, brainstorm the names of as many sea creatures as you can.

LIONFISH

The lionfish, also called the turkey fish, scorpion fish, or dragon fish, is found in tropical reefs around the world. It is a member of the scorpion fish family, a group of fish known for their long, poisonous spines. The lionfish swallows its prey whole. Don't get close to one of these! Their stings can be very painful.

SEA CREATURES

CUTTLEFISH

When is a fish not a fish? When it's a cuttlefish. A cuttlefish is actually a mollusk, which is in the same family as squid and octopuses. Cuttlefish are able to rapidly change skin color — from yellow to orange-red to blue-green. The patterns of skin flashes are a form of communication to other cuttlefish and help to camouflage them from predators. Cuttlefish have blue-green blood and three hearts! Two hearts pump blood to the gills, and the third heart pumps blood to the rest of the body.

camouflage: *disguise for protection*

OARFISH

The oarfish or ribbonfish is a very long, eel-like fish. It is in the *Guinness World Records* as the world's longest bony fish at more than 33 feet. There are some reports of oarfish reaching more than 50 feet long! These fish are seldom seen, but when they are, they are often mistaken for sea monsters.

CHECKPOINT

Check out the picture. Notice why it's called a ribbonfish.

NARWHAL

The narwhal is a small whale found in waters around the Canadian and the Russian Arctic. The male narwhal has a large spiraling tusk, which sticks out from its head like the tusk of a mythical unicorn. The tusk is used to fight other males for mating rights. The word narwhal means "corpse man" — a suitable name because it often swims or lies belly up in the water.

FANGTOOTH

This is one of the scariest looking deep-sea fish! Luckily, it grows only to about the size of a hand. The fangtooth feeds on fish using its large fangs. Its two biggest teeth are so large that when its mouth closes, these teeth slide into pockets in the roof of the mouth. The fangtooth lives worldwide in open water. There are two forms of this fish: a rounded form and a long, slender form.

ELECTRIC RAY

CHECKPOINT

Why is numb fish a good name?

Many people have heard of electric eels but not many know about electric rays. Sometimes called the numb fish, electric rays look like small stingrays and are able to generate strong electric charges. To stun their prey, these rays can give off repeated electric shocks of up to 220 volts — more than enough to knock a person over. Sometimes single shocks are much stronger. If you are deep-sea diving, steer clear of this one!

volts: *units of measurement for electricity*

JEWEL SQUID

The jewel squid is one of the strangest creatures found in the sea. The jewel squid's left eye is always much larger than its right eye. Some species have a left eye that is telescopic while the smaller right eye is not. Jewel squid hang in the water at an angle and use the larger eye to look up for passing prey. Meanwhile, the smaller eye looks below for any signs of attackers. The name "jewel" comes from the small, shiny spots found on the undersides of the body, head, and arms of the squid.

---

telescopic: *makes distant objects look closer*

Jewel squid–Getty Images/National Geographic/Brian J Skerry; Anglerfish–Getty Images/Taxi/John Seagrim; Coelacanth–Getty Images/Taxi/Peter Scoones; All Other Images–Shutterstock

ANGLERFISH

Anglerfish are also known as frogfish, goosefish, or monkfish. Ask for monkfish in a restaurant — it's ugly but tasty. The anglerfish has a huge head with sharp, pointed teeth and a small appendage that looks like a worm sticking out of its forehead. This lure has a faint glow, which helps attract small fish and shrimp from dark waters. Any curious prey that comes too close will quickly become dinner for a hungry anglerfish!

---

appendage: *something attached to something larger or more important*
lure: *decoy used to attract*

COELACANTH

Coelacanth (see-la-kanth) are older than dinosaurs. It was thought that they had become extinct more than 65 million years ago — until one was caught off the coast of South Africa in 1938. Some people call the coelacanth a living fossil. It's a huge fish, averaging 175 pounds. Since 1938, other coelacanths have been found off the eastern coast of Africa and in waters off northern Indonesia.

CHECKPOINT

Why do you think a fish this size was hard to find?

FYI

Most fish swim. The coffin fish walks. It uses its short fins to walk along the ocean floor.

wrap up

1. Create a three-column chart listing the name of each sea creature, other names that it has, and its most unusual feature.

2. Imagine that you are a reporter. Choose three of these sea creatures and write a catchy headline about a recent discovery for each one.

THE GREAT WHITE

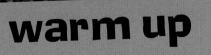

warm up

Look at the picture. Brainstorm words to describe a shark.

S ilently it slides
Through slippery black night
Beneath crashing waves
Which hide it from sight

Sweeping the depths
With midnight black eyes
Scanning for food
A morsel, a prize

It quickens its pace
As its hunger awakens
A prowling quest
For some prey to be taken

CHECKPOINT

What do you think this means?

The heartbeats get faster
Of the fish on the reef
As they shimmy and shake
In fear of those teeth!

Circling its prey
Now stricken with fright
Then off into darkness
A sated Great White.

---

morsel: *small piece of food*
stricken: *troubled*
sated: *filled with food*

Retell this poem in your own words.

Cool Facts

With a partner, brainstorm everything you know about sharks and dolphins.

There are more than 350 species of sharks in the world and many of them can be dangerous. Studies have shown, however, that there are three species responsible for most shark attacks. They are the great white shark, the tiger shark, and the bull shark. All three of these shark species are large predators that feed mainly on large fish, sea turtles, and marine mammals such as seals and dolphins.

Shovelnose shark

SHARKS

Shark Skin

The skin of a shark is very rough. It has many tiny bumps called denticles. Over the years, people have used it for many things, including sandpaper and nonslip grips for swords.

No Bones

Sharks are strong fish — perhaps the strongest fish in the sea. Even though sharks are strong, they do not have any bones in their bodies! The shark's body is supported entirely by cartilage, a tissue substance.

All Images–Shutterstock

14

About Sharks and Dolphins

FYI

The hammerhead shark has this name because its head is shaped like a hammer. Its eyes are found at the ends of the hammer. This allows it to see to the sides and react to danger or prey very quickly.

The Biggest Shark Ever!

With teeth as big as a human hand, the biggest shark that ever lived was called the megalodon. This huge shark was 40 to 50 feet long — three to four times bigger than the great white sharks of today!

CHECKPOINT

Great white sharks eat seals and walruses. What do you think a shark three times as big would eat?

Lots and Lots of Teeth

Sharks have many rows of teeth that are continually growing and replacing older teeth. This keeps the shark's teeth in very good condition. Sharks are always ready to pounce on a meal.

DOLPHINS

Sounding Off

Dolphins use sonar, or sound waves, to find their way through dark waters. The sonar that dolphins use is sent out from their heads. These sound waves travel outward and then bounce back to the dolphin, like a ball bouncing off a wall. They tell the dolphin all the things that are in front of it. Dolphins can sometimes really blast out their sound waves. This loud blast can actually stun smaller fish.

Dolphins Have Names

All dolphins have names. They even have their own sounds! When dolphins go exploring and want the other dolphins in their pod to know where they are or when they are coming back, they use their very own whistle — sort of like saying, "Hey! Over here! It's me!"

pod: *group of dolphins*

Tricky Sleepers

Dolphins need to breathe air every few minutes, so how do they sleep? Scientists have found that dolphins can put one half of their brain to sleep and keep the other half awake. This way, dolphins can get some rest, but still swim to the surface and get some air when they need to breathe. That's a pretty tricky way to sleep!

CHECKPOINT

Imagine what it would be like to get a good night's sleep but still know what's going on around you.

:FYI

- Bottlenose dolphins can swim at speeds of more than 18 miles per hour.

Two Stomachs

Dolphins actually have two stomachs. One is used to digest food, and the other is just a handy storage area. This allows dolphins to pack in food, just in case they get hungry later!

CHECKPOINT

Do you know of another animal that has more than one stomach?

Working Together

Dolphins live in large groups called pods. Most of the time, there are up to 20 dolphins in a pod, but sometimes dolphins form huge pods of up to 1,000. These pods of dolphins work as a team to circle around small groups of fish. Then they take turns rushing in and grabbing a mouthful. Dolphin pods often work together to chase away enemies, such as sharks, and sometimes they even kill sharks by smashing into them with their bills.

bills: *dolphins' beaks*

wrap up

1. If you could choose to be a shark or a dolphin, which one would you pick? Write a journal entry explaining which one you would rather be and why.

2. Many dolphins are killed each year by careless fishers, and shark numbers are quickly going down due to overfishing. Write a television news report about these problems and present it to the class.

WEB CONNECTIONS

Using a search engine, find out how sharks and dolphins are similar and different. Use a Venn diagram to present your findings.

A FISH STORY

Illustrated by Luke Markle

Paloma!" called her father. "Hurry up! We need your help loading the boat."

Paloma sighed. She hadn't been invited on the fishing trip. She quickly got dressed and combed her hair.

"Come on!" called her brother. "We have to be out past the reef in two hours."

The Pessoa family lived in a small village near the sea. They all loved to fish — including Paloma. Her fishing rod was her most treasured possession. Her grandfather had given it to her just before he died. It had a huge reel specifically designed to catch marlin. Her brother was still angry that he didn't get it, even though he already had two rods of his own.

Paloma always kept the reel clean and well-oiled in case she was allowed to go on one of her father's trips. She had gone on trips for other large fish, such as dorado, grouper, and even tuna — but never for marlin. Today was a trip for marlin.

possession: *personal belonging*
reel: *used for winding up or letting out fishing line*

"Come on, Paloma!" her brother shouted again.

Paloma walked out to the dock. She picked up the last few bags on the dock and loaded them onto the boat.

"Is that everything?" she asked her father.

"Where's your rod?" he asked with a smile.

Paloma couldn't believe her ears.

CHECKPOINT

What does this expression mean?

"My rod?" said Paloma, "Does that mean …?"

"Yes," replied her father. "You're coming marlin fishing with us."

Paloma quickly ran to get her things. She was back on the boat in a moment. With everything packed and stowed, the family headed toward the deep water beyond the reef.

"Now remember," her father said. "Marlin aren't like other fish. They're big, they're mean, and above all, they're strong."

---

stowed: *put away*

Paloma had heard many tales about her father's fishing adventures. Her father put fresh line on the reel, fastened it to the prized fishing rod and lowered the lure into the water. Her brother helped strap her into the fighting chair and attached the rod to the harness.

CHECKPOINT

Why do you think they did this?

"Today," began her father. "Today my daughter will catch her first marlin."

The minutes passed by very slowly. It had already been an hour and the fish weren't biting.

lure: *artificial bait used to catch fish*

They hadn't even seen any seabirds. Diving birds often meant small fish near the surface. Small fish often meant bigger fish.

Suddenly, Paloma's brother shouted, "A fin! I saw a huge fin just behind your lure!"

Paloma was ready for the fight to begin.

She turned to ask her father if he could see anything when suddenly her reel began to scream as line peeled off into the sea.

"Marlin!" screamed her brother.

"Marlin!" yelled her father.

:FYI

- There are different kinds of marlins.
- The Atlantic blue marlin is the largest.
- It can weigh more than 1,800 pounds!

Paloma held on tightly. The fish was very strong. If she hadn't been strapped into the fighting chair it would have pulled her overboard. She wanted to catch a marlin very badly, but she was afraid.

CHECKPOINT

Why do you think Paloma was afraid?

The rod was almost bent in half. The reel sang. She had never seen line disappear that fast. Suddenly, the fish jumped out of the water.

"It's huge!" cried her brother.

"It's going to jump again," said her father.

"Make sure you point the rod at it when it does."

It was very hot and sweat rolled down Paloma's face. She had only been fighting the fish for 15 minutes, but she was already tired. The reel was working perfectly. It was hard to hear her father's instructions over the screaming of the drag. Slowly, Paloma began to gain back some line. Her arms felt like they were being pulled down by lead weights.

"Are you tired? Do you want to give up?" asked her brother.

"No," replied Paloma. "I'm fine."

drag: *controls the tightness of the line on the reel*

But she wasn't fine. Her muscles ached like never before and the fish was still jumping and pulling at the line.

"Keep the rod up," said her father. "The fish is getting tired."

As much as Paloma's arms hurt, she knew her father was right. The fish was getting tired.

She could see it near the surface of the water.

It was the most beautiful thing she had ever seen.

"We'll have it soon!" screamed her father. "Don't let it dive."

Paloma began to feel sorry for the fish. She could tell it was as tired as she was. She wound in the line as fast as she could and tried to keep the rod up as her father had said. Her father and brother were looking over the side when suddenly there was a loud

PING!

as the line broke.

The fish was gone. Silence followed.

As the boat chugged toward the village, Paloma's father and brother wore sad frowns. Secretly, Paloma was happy. She knew her fish was free and would live to fight again. As they neared shore, Paloma turned one last time to look out toward the reef. It was a fishing trip she would never forget.

wrap up

1. Why do you think Paloma was secretly happy that her fish got away? What do you think was the most important part of the trip? Share your answers with a partner.

2. Imagine you are a newspaper reporter. Write a short report about Paloma's adventure. Include an exciting headline.

Mythical of the Deep

warm up

Have you ever read or been told stories about mythical creatures? Share what you know with a partner.

There are many stories about mythical sea creatures. Often these stories come about because people are afraid of what they cannot see in dark water.

Cadborosaurus

A famous Canadian sea serpent is Cadborosaurus. It is also called Caddy. Caddy has been talked about in native communities for hundreds of years. Today, many people from British Columbia believe it is real, but most scientists disagree.

Caddy is reported as being 15 to 50 feet long with a very long neck. Sometimes it is mistaken for the Loch Ness monster, which is an unexplained sea creature from Scotland. Caddy is snake-like in appearance and has fins or flippers so that it can swim very fast. Many believers think Caddy can swim as fast as 25 miles per hour.

Cadborosaurus by Mike Rooth

Creatures

Mermaids

Mermaid stories have come from all over the world, especially from Greek, Caribbean, European, and Japanese cultures.

Mermaids are said to be beautiful women who are part fish — the bottom halves of their bodies are scaly fish tails. Because they are part fish, mermaids are said to be able to survive underwater. Sailors have reported seeing mermaids while at sea. Many of these sailors were away from their loved ones for long periods of time. It is possible that what they were really seeing were manatees, sea creatures that move very slowly.

CHECKPOINT

There are many stories about mermaids. Can you think of one?

A Mermaid
by John William Waterhouse

25

The Midgard Serpent

This sea serpent was known to Scandinavians as a sworn enemy of Thor, the god of thunder. Sometimes the Midgard Serpent was called the World Serpent. It had to live in the ocean because it could not stop growing! The Midgard Serpent grew so long it circled Earth and its tail was able to reach into its mouth!

Many Scandinavians tell the story of a battle between Thor and the Midgard Serpent. Thor used his hammer to kill the creature, but then died from the serpent's poison.

Thor and Hymir go fishing for the Midgard Serpent.

Midgard Serpent–from the 18th century Icelandic manuscript SÁM 66 in the care of the Árni Magnússon Institute in Iceland.

Sirens

Sirens look like mermaids, but they are different creatures — described as half-bird and half-woman. They are said to live on rocky islands and were first mentioned in Greek myths. Sirens are said to lure sailors and their boats

lure: *attract*

close to rocks with their beautiful singing. The sailors then crash into the rocks and drown!

Sirens are mentioned in a popular story called *The Odyssey*. In this story, Odysseus, an adventurous ship captain, ordered his men to put beeswax in their ears so they could not be lured by singing sirens!

Ulysses and the Sirens by John William Waterhouse

- FYI

There are about
500 different species
of squid. Some can
grow to be as large
as a school bus.

Kraken

Kraken attacking a ship

Ever since people started exploring the seas in boats, kraken have been one of the most feared beasts. Kraken look like huge octopuses because they have many tentacles. They have been described as being as big as an island and are often shown in old paintings wrapped around large sailing vessels. In some paintings, kraken are tossing sailors into their mouths.

Sightings of kraken were probably just exaggerated sightings of giant squid, which are very large sea creatures with eight arms and two tentacles.

tentacles: *long parts of an animal used to grab or touch things*
exaggerated: *made bigger than usual*

wrap up

1. Many scientists do not believe in mythical sea creature sightings. With a partner, discuss what kinds of evidence they would need in order to believe in these stories.

2. Make up your own sea creature and draw a picture of it. Write a short description of what it looks like, how big it is, what it eats, where it lives, and who its enemies are.

WEB CONNECTIONS

Use the Web to find another mythical creature not mentioned in this article. List three interesting facts about it.

THE BIGGEST
... and Other WACKy Facts

warm up

With a partner, share any unusual facts you know about sea creatures.

The Earth's oceans are filled with many strange and wonderful creatures. Ever wonder what the fastest fish in the sea is? Or which creature has the biggest eyes? Find out the answer to these questions and lots more!

The Fastest Fish in the Sea

The fastest fish in the sea are sailfish. These large open-sea predators have long bills sticking out from their mouths and dorsal fins that look like big, fan-like sails. Sailfish use their long bills to stun and injure their prey by slashing through schools of smaller fish. Sailfish then circle back to gobble an easy meal.

There are several other fish that can swim very fast. The mako is the fastest shark in the ocean, with a top speed of almost 25 miles per hour. This predator is very strong and often jumps right out of the water while chasing its prey.

EYES ON EARTH

Watch Out for Shocks!

Some sea creatures, like electric eels found in freshwater, can make their own electricity! Electric rays make electricity from special cells within their bodies. These cells are lined up in rows along their backs like a row of batteries all connected together.

Weird Blood

Did you know that some fish have blood that doesn't freeze? The Arctic cod and some fish from the Antarctic Ocean have this type of blood. This helps them survive in their frigid undersea habitats.

---

frigid: *very cold*

Longest Teeth

The longest teeth are not found on well-known predators like sharks. They are found on narwhals, small whales living in the Arctic Ocean. The tusk of the male narwhal is actually one of its teeth, which gets longer as the male matures. Female narwhals have two regular teeth that stay in their mouths. They do not form tusks.

29

The Slowest Fish in the Sea

The sea horse is the slowest fish in the sea. It would take a sea horse more than two and a half days to swim one mile! Sea horses also have strange families — the male sea horse has the babies! Now that is a wacky fact!

THE LARGEST ...

EYES It is very dark in the deepest parts of the sea. The creatures that live there have big eyes, which help them see without any light. Big eyes help creatures watch out for predators or find their prey. The giant squid, which lives in the deepest parts of the ocean, has the biggest eyes of any creature on Earth. They are bigger than volleyballs and help the squid see in almost total darkness.

CHECKPOINT
The giant squid can see very well in the dark. What land animals can see well in the dark?

CRAB Most people think crabs are rather small, but did you know there is a crab that is as wide as a car? The giant Japanese spider crab has a claw span (the width from the tip of the longest leg to the tip of the other) of more than ten feet!

The Deepest Fish in the Deepest Water

The deepest parts of the sea are found in trenches, which are splits in the sea floor that look like canyons. The deepest fish ever found was the cusk eel, which was found in the Puerto Rico Trench — more than three miles below the surface!

WHALE The largest whale ever found was a female blue whale captured off the Shetland Islands in 1926. It was more than 98 feet long and weighed about 187 tons. A whale that big would be able to hold about seven minivans end to end or 60 people standing side by side! The blue whale is the largest animal that has ever lived. It's even bigger than any of the largest-known dinosaurs!

wrap up

1. With a partner, use the unusual facts in this selection to make up a true-or-false quiz. Give the quiz to others in your class or group.

2. Choose the most interesting or unusual fact and create a labeled diagram to explain it.

Do They

Ever Land?

All Images—Shtterstock/iStockphoto

warm up

There are many types of seabirds. In a small group, see how many different kinds you can name.

When most people think of sea creatures, birds are usually not the first creatures that come to mind. But there is a bird that spends its entire life at sea. Meet the albatross.

In many ways, the albatross is unusual among birds. It spends almost the entire year at sea, either flying over it or swimming and diving for food.

The wandering albatross, which can live more than 60 years, is the biggest of all the albatross species. It has the biggest wingspan of any bird in the world — more than ten feet tip to tip. An adult male can weigh more than 25 pounds, which is more than twice the weight of most eagles. Albatrosses are incredible flyers. Some scientists believe they are such good flyers that they could travel around the entire world without ever stopping!

Albatrosses are found in bodies of water in many places around the world, but they prefer more distant areas of the open water, which is where they find their food.

Their food is usually shrimp, small fish, and sometimes floating dead sea animals. Because of their great flying ability, albatrosses will sometimes fly more than 1,250 miles in a day to find a meal.

The only time an albatross will actually come back to land is to breed. Once a male albatross and a female albatross become a mating pair, they stay together for life. The female usually lays only a single egg at a time.

Once the chick hatches and grows big enough to head out to sea with its parents, it is often up to 10 years before it ever returns to land.

For many years, details of the daily life of the albatross have been a mystery. However, scientists have recently started using satellite technology to track the movements of albatrosses. What scientists have found out is truly astonishing!

It seems that when an albatross is trying to feed its young, it will sometimes fly over the seas for up to two weeks searching for food. Also, an albatross can actually sleep while it's flying!

CHECKPOINT

Two weeks is a long time to wait for dinner! How long do you think you could go before you absolutely had to eat something?

Another interesting fact is that an albatross doesn't have to spend any energy to keep its wings spread out. Researchers have discovered that an albatross can lock its wings in the stretched-out position. An albatross actually uses less energy when it is flying than when it is sitting on the ground!

The albatross is truly an amazing sea creature, but its future is in doubt. Sadly, the albatross is now facing extinction and soon there may be no more. One reason is that, for over the last 20 years, fishers have been using long lines to try to catch more fish. These long lines can be several miles long and they have a hook attached every 20 inches. These hooks not only catch fish but also many seabirds, including albatrosses. Once hooked, not very many birds are able to escape and most drown.

extinction: *dying out*

Because albatrosses raise only one chick and breed only every two to three years, their numbers are quickly getting smaller. Many people around the world are trying to save these wonderful birds.

People are always amazed when they find out more about albatrosses. Only by educating more people will we be able to save the bird that hardly ever lands.

wrap up

1. What is the most interesting fact you discovered about albatrosses? Share your opinion in a small group.

2. The albatross is an amazing sea creature, but it is in danger of extinction. Give a speech that explains why the albatross is in danger and what people can do to help save it.

WEB CONNECTIONS

Go online to find four or five different types of seabirds. Make a list of these and note the ones you have seen.

WHALES AND MARINE

An Interview with an

Image Of Jim Darling–Courtesy Of Jim Darling; All Other Images–Shutterstock/iStockphoto

warm up

Why do you think researching marine life is important?

Dr. Jim Darling

Beluga whale

Dr. Jim Darling travels the world to study whales. Dr. Darling and other researchers make up the Pacific Wildlife Foundation, a **charitable** coastal and marine research and education group. Dr. Darling and his group have taught the world a great deal about whales and other marine animals.

charitable: *freely giving money or help*

36

ANIMALS: Expert

Bottlenose dolphin

BOLDPRINT: Marine mammals are thought to be very intelligent. What do you think?

JIM DARLING: This is a very common question, but not a simple one to answer. Bottlenose dolphins have large brains compared to the size of their bodies. They are generally thought to be very intelligent. Most of the other marine mammals we are familiar with, including all the seals, sea lions, and large whales, do not have large brains in relation to their body sizes, so are not likely to be any more intelligent than other mammals. It is difficult, if not impossible, to compare the intelligence of one species to another.

BP: How smart are marine mammals compared to other animals, such as gorillas, monkeys, dogs, or cats?

JD: Most researchers would agree that bottlenose dolphins, killer whales, and perhaps some of the other dolphin species are as smart as the non-human primates, such as chimpanzees and gorillas. Most whales and other marine mammals might be closer to the intelligence level of a dog or horse.

CHECKPOINT

What are some smart things that animals can do?

BP: Do whales live in families?

JD: Yes and no. There are more than 80 species of whales and dolphins and each has its own social organization or grouping. For example, some killer whales live in families and stay with their family group throughout their lives. Many other toothed whales, including dolphins, live in larger groups and communities, but there is some movement from one group to another. The larger baleen whales do not live in family groups; they live in a social group that may sometimes resemble a herd, similar to some land mammals like buffalo or caribou.

BP: Do you think that people will one day be able to communicate or "talk" to whales?

JD: It seems unlikely that this will occur, beyond the shared "language" dolphins have with trainers or with scientists who are studying them.

CHECKPOINT

Why do you think the word "language" is in quotation marks?

The time when we can hold conversations with whales, much like we do with other humans, is at best a long way off.

Black whale

Killer whales

All Images—Shutterstock/iStockphoto

BP: What are whales doing when they "sing"?

JD: A song is a series of sounds repeated over and over. The most famous whale singers are humpback whales. In this case, the males sing during the breeding season, and they sing until joined by other males (not females). We do not know why they sing, but it seems to play a role in organizing males during the breeding season.

BP: What kind of education and training do you need to become a whale researcher?

JD: Most researchers are educated as biologists at a college or university. It helps to have knowledge about photography and have experience with boats and working on (and in) the ocean.

---

biologists: *scientists who study living things*

Humpback whale

BP: What is the most rewarding part of your job at Pacific Wildlife Foundation?

JD: The most rewarding part is learning new things — having the research lead to new knowledge about whales, which we then share with the world. I also love being in a boat far out on the ocean with the whales.

BP: If you could find out one new thing about whales, what would it be?

JD: This is a tough question to answer — there are so many! I would like to learn how whales keep close relationships in the huge oceans, and especially how they use sound to talk to each other.

wrap up

Researching whales and marine animals can be a very exciting job. Write a short story about an adventure you might have if you were at sea researching whales.

BACK AT THE LAB ... WITH THE TRACKING DEVICE SECURELY ATTACHED TO THE SHARK, THE TEAM WATCHES THE SHARK'S MOVEMENT ON COMPUTER MONITORS.

GREAT JOB, TEAM. WE'RE GETTING SOME *AMAZING* INFORMATION!

YEAH! I DIDN'T KNOW TIGER SHARKS HAD SUCH A LARGE TERRITORY.

AND IT ALMOST DIDN'T WORK!

MAYBE NEXT TIME WE SHOULD TRY SOME MAYO WITH THAT TUNA!

OH GEEZ!

... WHY AM I HUNGRY ALL OF A SUDDEN?

FYI

Scientists track sharks to view their habits and find out about the areas of the ocean that they visit. This will help them figure out why some species of sharks are in danger of becoming extinct. Tracking also helps scientists figure out why some species attack humans.

Many other sea creatures, such as dolphins, tuna, sea turtles, and seals, have also been tracked by scientists.

wrap up

1. As one of the scientists, write an e-mail to a friend or fellow scientist describing the problems with attaching the tracking device to the shark.

2. If you could track any sea creature, which creature would you pick? Why? Share your choice with a partner.

43

AN EEL'S JOURNEY

American eel

American eel ... © Stuart Pearce / AgePics.com; All Other Images—Shutterstock/iStockphoto

warm up

What words do you think of when you hear the word "eel"? Share your thoughts with a partner.

The eel is one of the most mysterious creatures found in the sea. Many people find them frightening and stay away from them. Other people, however, think they make a delicious meal. Eels are found in most of the oceans of the world and even far inland. In ancient times, people had no idea where eels came from. The great philosopher Aristotle believed eels came from earthworms and simply popped out of wet soil. In the Middle Ages, eels were thought to come from other eel-like fish, such as the eelpout, a completely different kind of fish!

philosopher: *person who seeks wisdom and understanding about life*

It was not until the early 1900s that scientists finally proved that American eels were a separate species of fish that grew from tiny larvae to full-size eels up to eight feet long.

Still, the mystery remained. Where did they come from? No breeding of American eels had ever been seen. It often seemed that, one day, there would be no eels and then, the next day, all of a sudden, people would start catching them in nets or on a fishing line far up a river — where they hadn't been before!

Today, we know that all American eels of the world originated in a small area in the Atlantic Ocean called the Sargasso Sea, which is found just south of the island of Bermuda.

From this small area of the ocean, American eels traveled great distances and spread around the world. In fact, they have often been found very far from the ocean in places like Lake Ontario or the Mississippi River.

larvae: *stage of development before fully grown*

originated: *started; began*

Other Types of Eels

White-eye eel

CHECKPOINT

Do you think there are any eels in a river or lake close to your home?

Snowflake eel

Other Types of Eels

Ribbon eel

Giant moray eel

American eels begin their lives as tiny larvae, which are almost see-through. Their great journeys to faraway rivers and lakes involve drifting in ocean currents, until they grow to three to four inches long and have enough strength to swim for themselves. These tiny eels, called elvers, can take many years to find their way to freshwater. Once they reach the river mouths, the males usually stay in the area, while the females start their journey upstream.

As the eels make their way upstream, they change in color from silvery gray to a light yellow. They grow slowly over a period of 10 to 15 years, and end up in some very out-of-the-way places. For many years, rumors of eels in small ponds and lakes, far from any river, were not believed.

How could a creature that was born in the middle of the ocean end up in a small inland lake or pond? At first, scientists thought that for some strange reason people must have walked to some of these small inland waters, taking the eels with them, and then letting them go. The truth of the matter was even stranger — the eels themselves did the walking!